HOW TO DRAW
FISHING CRAFT

by STUART E. BECK

THE STUDIO PUBLICATIONS
London & New York

First published 1953

Published in London by The Studio Limited,
66 Chandos Place, W.C.2, and in New York by
Studio Publications Inc., 432 Fourth Avenue
and printed in England by Bradford & Dickens,
Drayton House, London, W.C.1

CONTENTS

Introduction   4

A study in curves   6

Constructional sketches   8

Superstructure   14

Outdoor sketching hints   16

Faults to avoid   19

How to start a sketch   23

Distance and atmosphere   24

Tone without lines   28

Movement   30

Methods of fishing   33

Types of craft :   38

    STEAM AND MOTOR TRAWLERS
    SPANISH 'PAREJA' TRAWLER
    DUTCH CRAFT
    HASTINGS LUGGER
    STEAM DRIFTERS
    BAWLEYS
    BRIXHAM SMACKS
    CONCARNEAU TUNNYMAN
    SEINE NET FISHERS
    WITH THE WHALERS
    NEWFOUNDLAND BANKS SCHOONERS

Surroundings   58

Sketching outfits   60

Fishing ports   62

Conclusion   63

INTRODUCTION

FROM an artist's point of view, perhaps no ships offer so much interest, grace of line or richness of colour as the many types of fishing craft. Whether under sail or power, each possesses her own particular character, from deep sea vessels such as the Newfoundland Banks schooners and powerful modern Icelandic trawlers to the stout little inshore shrimpers.

Quite apart from the boats themselves there is much good material in the bronzed faces and stalwart figures of the fisher-folk, while snug harbours, where weatherbeaten craft lie at their moorings, make a perfect background for the main subject of our book.

The artist of to-day must resign himself to the fact that sails have practically vanished from the sea and have been replaced by steam or motor engines. There are, however, still a few of the older boats in commission fitted with auxiliary power, so although it may no longer be possible to see them under sail, their hulls, rigging and deck gear can be studied at first hand. By sketches of these boats and the help of early photographs or drawings one can reconstruct them as they appeared in their sailing days.

No true artist likes slavishly copying a photograph or another man's work, so it is well worth studying a craft from all angles to get a clear conception of her lines. The set of the sails, details of rigging and the heeling of a boat under various conditions of wind and sea require careful research to enable the artist to work out his own interpretation of a fishing vessel at work.

Now what about the craft's natural element, the sea ? This is bound to feature in many of your sketches and is probably among the most difficult things to draw. There are hints and tips on the subject in other books of this series so I do not propose to say much about it, although the sea is shown in various moods in some of my sketches. As a matter of fact I do not think it possible to *teach* very much about drawing such a constantly moving and changeable subject. It is persistent observation, practice and enthusiasm which will most improve your work.

Talking about enthusiasm, provided you have an aptitude for drawing, this probably has more influence on your progress than any other single factor. Without it nobody will get very far. Take, for example, two artists of exactly equal ability. There is one fellow who is keen enough to visit a nearby port occasionally on a fine Saturday afternoon and sketch for a couple of hours. There is another who, in January, travels on the midnight train to a distant harbour so as to arrive by dawn and make the most of the daylight. Boarding the evening train for home, cold to the marrow and dead tired, he is soon asleep, but on the rack above his head is the best sketch he has ever done. This is the hundred per cent enthusiasm that will surmount many obstacles given up as hopeless by the first man. Let enthusiasm and perseverance be your watchwords.

It now only remains for us to pick up our sketching gear, cast off our moorings and get under way.

Bound for the Fishing Grounds

A STUDY IN CURVES

FISHING craft, taken as a whole probably contain more curves in their make up than any other class of vessel. Therefore the artist who wishes to draw them accurately must take a great deal of trouble to master this feature of his subject. Of course there are plenty of people who make very attractive pictures of fishing smacks in harbours without really attempting to draw the boats properly. These sketches may be first-class in colour, composition and painting technique, but do not convey any idea of the true character of the craft.

In a plan view the sides of a ship curve in to the bow and stern, and you must never lose sight of the fact that the two sides are always symmetrical. This point is apt to be forgotten when drawing a vessel from unusual angles.

A side elevation will show a more

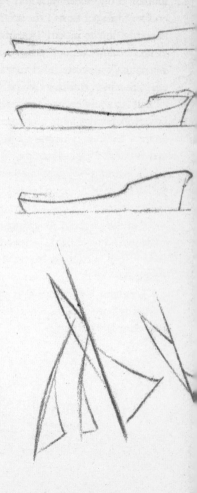

or less pronounced curve in the deck line from bow to stern. This is known as the Sheer Line and varies according to the type of craft.

The ' bilges,' that is the angles where the sides meet the bottom of the ship, are rounded. The complete hull is a combination of all the curves mentioned and many more, blended into one another to give minimum resistance in its passage through the water, while preserving the necessary qualities of stability, carrying capacity and other requirements. Superstructure details such as modern rounded bridge fronts, funnel tops etc, all present their curve problems, while sails are a mass of subtle curves which vary according to their cut, their angle and the strength of the wind.

CONSTRUCTIONAL SKETCHES

T H E subject of this little book is how to draw fishing craft—*not* how to draw. That would require many very large books indeed. We will suppose, therefore, that you have already done some pencil, pen or colour sketching and that you know something about perspective. Those who are ' all at sea ' over perspective will find some useful hints on it in *How to Draw Perspectives* by W. H. Fuller (Studio Publications).

Although you may have a good idea of general perspective, fishing craft, as already stated, contain so many curves that it may be as well to kick off with a few constructional sketches. First of all let us develop the hull of a steam trawler from a ' box.'

The most important items in the process are longitudinal centre lines at deck level and keel. This is because, the ship being symmetrical, the hull curves are the same each side. Also practically all superstructure and deck fittings are either on or equidistant from the deck centre line. The keel is the ' backbone ' from which the curved ribs grow to produce the under-water form of the ship.

Should you be drawing a craft afloat from a fairly high view-point, the centre line at water level must be susbsituted for the keel line. Now draw a transparent ' box ' whose apparent length is about six times its breadth. Draw centre lines along top and bottom, and join them by verticals at each end, figure 1.

You will remember my mention of ' sheer ' and this must be added by converting the three top straight lines into smooth curves, figure 2. We now have the deck plane A B C D on which must be drawn the deck shape. Draw six lines across the deck, sketch in the rounded stern, and the bow curves which are at the near end of the box extending back to about the second crossline, figure 3.

This bow shape (shaded) I have christened the ' flatiron ' because it is so like the base of an ordinary domestic iron as shown in the thumb-nail sketches. In fact you could quite well use one as a model by propping it up at various angles, possibly with a centre line marked on it. The near centre vertical line would represent the stem or sharp edge of the bow in an old steam trawler, but in modern vessels the stem is raked, that is it slopes back from deck to keel, so our stem line will cross the keel line a little way back from the end of the box.

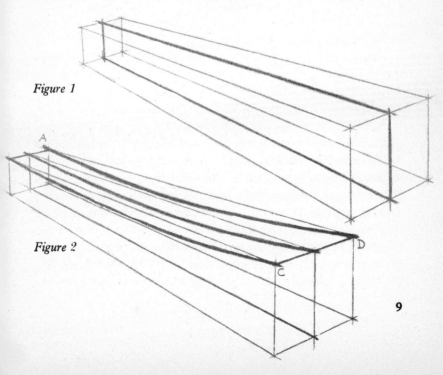

Figure 1

Figure 2

9

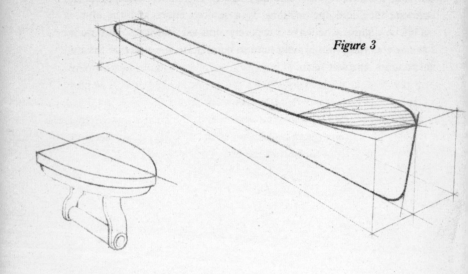

Figure 3

When the angle between stem and keel lines has been rounded off we have practically all the basic hull outline except its girth or 'fullness.' This is easy enough to sketch in from the actual ship or, after a good deal of practice, from memory, but at this stage let's make use of cross sections. Suppose we have a solid wooden model of a trawler's hull. Now imagine that we mark it off and cut it through at equal intervals like slicing a loaf. Scarcely any two of these slices will be alike. The ones in the middle will be roughly like a letter ' U.' Those towards the bow will become gradually ' V ' shaped, and towards the stern more like

a ' Y,' figure 4. Returning to the ' box ' drawing, drop a vertical from
the centre of each cross line and lightly sketch in the appropriate
sections, then join the sections by a smooth curve and the ship is
complete, figure 5. I have purposely omitted bulwarks and raised
forecastle as these would only tend to complicate the study of the hull
shape in its simplest form.

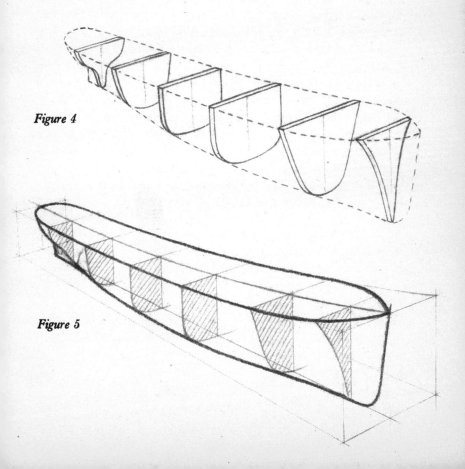

Figure 4

Figure 5

Some trawlers when afloat are much higher out of the water forward than aft. In other words the keel is not horizontal but sloping downwards towards the stern, figure 6. So if you want to make a constructional drawing of the part of the hull which is above water your box will have to taper downwards towards one end, and the lower centre line will be at water level. On the opposite page are several sketches from various angles, with the old flat iron still coming in useful. Figure 7 is practically the same as figure 3 except that it shows only the upper part of the hull. A high viewpoint drawing from astern is shown in figure 8, a low level stern view in figure 9 and a low level bow view in figure 10.

Although these diagrams are applied to a modern trawler, the principle would be just as suitable for sailing trawlers, drifters or, for that matter, any other type of ship.

I must mention here that the diagrams are not necessarily accurate in proportion or hull form, but are sketched simply to show the skeleton upon which to build up a sound drawing. With experience you will be able to dispense with the ' skeleton ' and sketch in your outline straight away with reasonable accuracy, or at any rate only indicate one or two of the main construction lines as a guide.

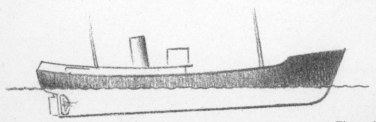

Figure 6

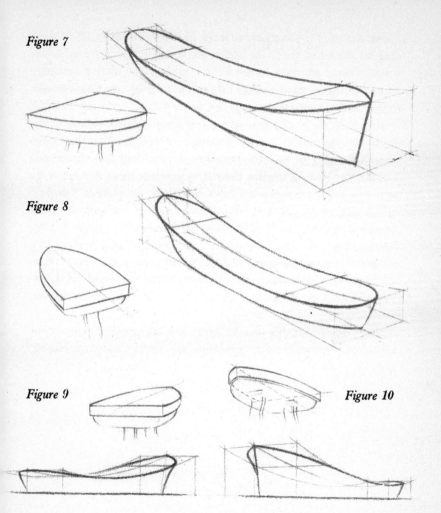

Figure 7

Figure 8

Figure 9

Figure 10

SUPERSTRUCTURE

HAVING drawn the simple hull shape, our next job is to add bulwarks, raised forecastle and superstructure.

I am sorry to inflict a few more constructional details on you before we launch out into the realms of really free sketching, but these principles of drawing can be applied to any type of craft and a good foundation will pay in the long run. In most large modern trawlers there is the raised forecastle—roughly corresponding with the ' flatiron ' shape—and a long deckhouse extending from amidships towards the stern, leaving a clear foredeck. Sometimes this house ends a short distance from the stern, allowing a small boat to be stowed on deck. Sometimes it is carried right to the stern, where it is extended to the vessel's sides and covered with a short deck accommodating two boats on davits. Superimposed on the forward end of the deckhouse is the bridge and wheelhouse.

When laying out this superstructure it is important to position the various parts centrally on the hull. This can best be ensured by stepping

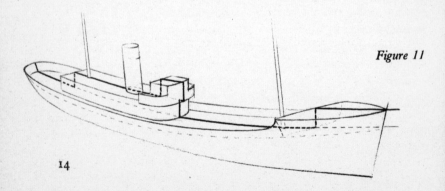

Figure 11

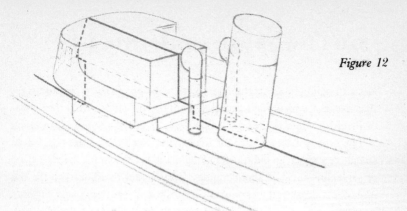

Figure 12

Figure 13

up the main deck centre line as required, figure 11. Figure 12 is another view showing part of the deckhouse and bridge, with placing of the funnel and ventilators, from a slightly astern angle. You will see how the bridge and funnel are on the centre line of the deckhouse top, while the two ventilators are equidistant from it.

In the example the wheelhouse front is not vertical but sloping back slightly. This is a common practice among British trawlers to-day. Another feature of many of these ships is a rounded stem on the forecastle deck plan, gradually tapering to a sharp edge at the waterline. This adds yet another small curve to our list, and is quite tricky to draw correctly in perspective. Examples of the round stem from two angles are given in figure 13.

OUTDOOR SKETCHING HINTS

O NE thing about sketching fishing craft—or any other type of ship for that matter—which may catch the beginner off his guard is the movement of his subject. Ships and boats are not static like houses or trees.

The artist visiting a harbour may spend some time searching for an attractive subject, an old trawler alongside a quay perhaps. After a period of sketching out it is about midday. He decides to adjourn to the old town for a drink and a sandwich. Refreshed, he hurries back, eager to start colouring the pencil sketch, only to find that his trawler is now several miles out at sea ! In place of an interesting composition and wonderful colour there lies before him a barren expanse of empty quayside. A few discreet enquiries from one of the trawlermen or a local bystander, before starting, would probably have informed him that the ship was about to sail, and he could have speeded up his work accordingly or chosen another subject.

Tides also affect the movement of craft in river or harbour and must be taken into account. Once, many years ago, I settled down to make a careful detailed drawing of a small vessel alongside a harbour wall. The subject was rather like that shewn below. After a time there appeared to be something wrong with my drawing. The rim round the funnel top,

which had been curved as it was well above my eye level, seemed to have become straighter. The deck line which had been about half way between quay and the top of the ship's bridge was now only a quarter of the way up. In a moment or two I realised that the ship was slowly falling with the ebb tide, and it was not so very long before only masts, funnel, bridge and forecastle were visible !

In shallow water, the sailing smack you are drawing is perhaps afloat, but as the tide goes down she will rest on the bottom showing an unnatural amount of her hull above water. If the tide falls so low that the harbour bed dries out, then a deep keeled vessel will heel over at an acute angle, resting on one bilge. There are diagrams illustrating these points on the next page.

Should you want to make a drawing of a vessel anchored in a tidal river or harbour, it is advisable to commence work just after the beginning of the flood or ebb tide. About the times of high water and low water a ship normally swings round her anchor as the current changes from flow to ebb or vice versa. Therefore, if you start sketching a vessel broadside on for example, half an hour before high water, it will not be long before her angle begins to alter until an end-on view confronts you. From then on she will continue to swing and eventually present a broadside view once more, but now the ship is heading in the opposite direction and has moved some distance either up or down stream.

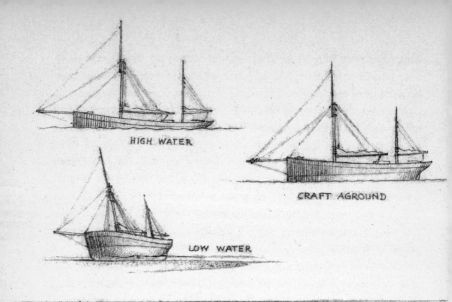

HIGH WATER

CRAFT AGROUND

LOW WATER

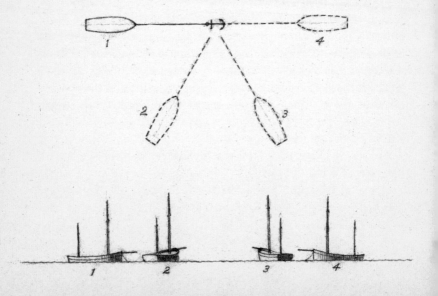

1   2   3   4

FAULTS TO AVOID

THERE are countless mistakes that can be made in the drawing of ships. Almost every detail in an extremely complicated structure may be either wrongly drawn or—which is quite as bad—drawn out of its proper position. Do not think from this statement that I am necessarily in favour of photographic accuracy in the presentation of a subject. The amount of liberty that may be taken with the drawing depends on what you are aiming at. If you intend your picture to be a faithful portrait of a particular vessel or type, then to my mind the greatest possible accuracy is essential. On the other hand, in a sketch which is a characteristic impression of a vessel or group of craft I think a certain degree of distortion or exaggeration is permissible and even an advantage in some cases.

To use an 'Irish' expression, there is a form of 'right wrongness' which may give extra life, interest and possibly improved composition to a picture, but it requires a good deal of experience and sound personal judgment if you are not to stray over the borderline into 'wrong wrongness.' Should the craft you are drawing have a particularly tall funnel, by making it a little taller still you may improve the sketch as a character study, without breaking any of the fundamental rules of ship construction. But supposing you were to draw a trawler with her funnel off the centre line, or a smack with her sails set in such a way that the wind must be blowing from two directions at the same time, you would be guilty of a real 'howler'!

A few of the more common faults are illustrated on the following pages. Figure 14 shows the 'twisted hull' : you will see that while the line across the deck at the stern is more or less level, the ' flatiron ' is tilted over to one side. Figure 15 shows more correct drawing. Funnel tops are a bit tricky in perspective, as the funnel depends for its correct appearance mainly upon the curve of its top rim being just right. In figure 16 the rim is drawn straight, although the funnel is sloping back in perspective. It looks as though it is falling over towards us. Figure 17 shows the top curved, giving the funnel its proper apparent angle of rake.

Bridge fronts need careful drawing in perspective, because if the top

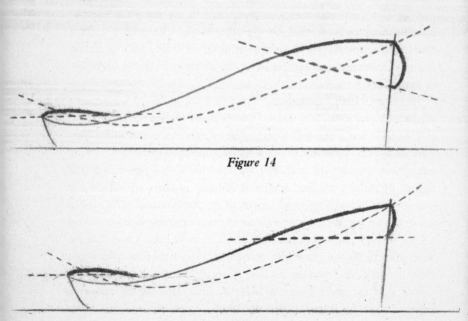

Figure 14

Figure 15

20

Figure 16   Figure 17

and bottom lines are not at the correct angle the bridge will look as if
it is sloping down towards one side, or is not placed squarely on the
centre line. Two wrong versions, one sloping down and the other up
too much, are illustrated in figure 18.

Lastly, the bow in perspective. One sees many sketches with the
far side drawn like the upper diagram in figure 19. But if you remember
the flatiron shape it should be easy enough to achieve a more correct
line as shewn in the lower diagram.

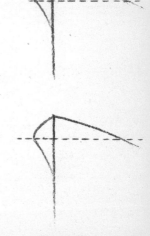

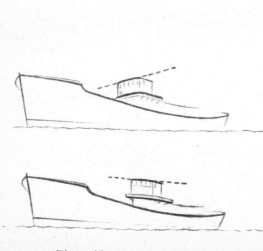

Figure 18   Figure 19

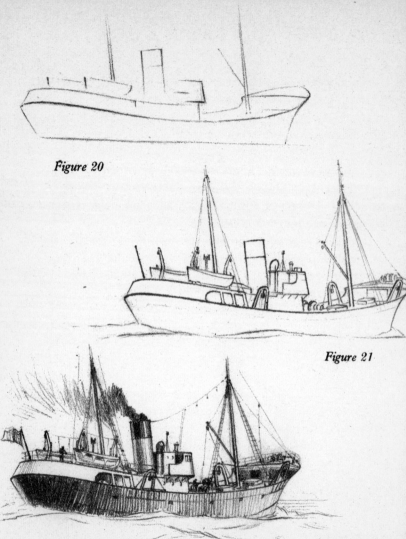

Figure 20

Figure 21

Figure 22

HOW TO START A SKETCH

THE making of a good sketch depends largely on the method of working, quite apart from your keen observation and skill in actual drawing. It is important to know how to start, because when taking your first look at a fishing vessel you may be ' dazzled ' and confused by the amount of complicated detail.

One sometimes sees a beginner attempting a subject of this kind commence his drawing near one edge of the paper and laboriously work along to the other end of the ship, putting in all the detail as he goes. without any preliminary laying out.

This method nearly always results in an extremely fussy sketch which is hideously out of proportion. Before beginning to draw you should study your subject for two or three minutes, and in imagination strip the vessel of all detail, leaving only the essential basic lines.

Having done this and worked out the main proportions of the ship, then, and then only, is it time to start drawing, in the form of a light sketch of the whole craft, figure 20. The next step is to strengthen up the drawing and add the main details, figure 21. Complete the sketch by putting in as much small detail as you like and any shading required, figure 22. Your work may range from drawings showing every bit of gear carefully drawn, to the barest impression of a craft in one or two tones painted with a large brush, without any preliminary drawing at all. But remember that to be just right the simple impression often needs more skill and knowledge than the complicated, highly finished drawing. It is no easy matter to leave out so much without losing the character of the subject.

DISTANCE AND ATMOSPHERE

THERE are three main things which give the effect of distance in a drawing. First of all there is the comparative size of objects ; secondly the relative position of objects, and thirdly their difference in tone.

The four diagrams on the opposite page show two ships which, in real life are the same size and colour, and we want to form them into a picture with one vessel fairly near and the other far away.

In figure 23 one trawler is drawn much smaller than the other, as objects look smaller at a distance, but both being positioned at the same level below the horizon line, it simply appears to be a little ship alongside a big one.

Figure 24 shows one vessel positioned nearer the horizon line and thus ' further away ' in linear perspective, but as they are both drawn the same size the effect is wrong.

In figure 25 the tone of the two ships is different, but being drawn the same size and the same distance below the horizon line, they just look like one grey painted vessel and one black.

None of these arrangements is satisfactory, but in figure 26 where all three things are combined, the two craft immediately take up their proper relative ' depth ' in the picture.

A more realistic example of this aspect of drawing is illustrated on the two following pages. There are two sketches showing a line of drifters returning to harbour. In the first, all the craft are more or less solid black ; on the facing page the tones are graduated from the nearest to the most distant vessel. This produces a pleasing effect of distance and that hazy atmosphere so often seen on a fine summer morning or evening

24

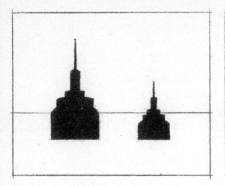

Figure 23

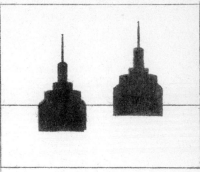

Figure 24

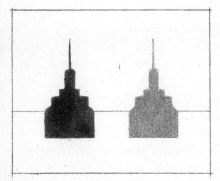

Figure 25

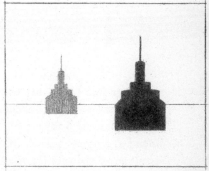

Figure 26

Another hint which may help in this matter of distance and atmosphere concerns your treatment of detail.

When drawing a subject containing perhaps several craft and background at varying distances from the artist, the details of the nearest vessel can be shown fully, in crisp light and shade.

Then, as you move to the more distant objects, you can subdue or leave out more and more detail. A plain flat shape in tone will probably suffice for treatment of the extreme background, unless it has some particular interest.

Many sketches are spoilt by being cluttered up with a lot of bits and pieces which only detract from the picture as a whole.

In seeming contradiction of these remarks, there is a type of line drawing in which everything is elaborately detailed, regardless of distance. This style relies upon perfect drawing and placing of objects in linear perspective for its effect of distance. Also the treatment of near craft is usually bold and heavy, the thickness of lines being gradually reduced as the more distant parts of the subject are reached.

TONE WITHOUT LINES

WHEN the drawing of various craft has been thoroughly mastered in pencil line one can begin to have fun experimenting with different treatments.

One possible method is to make a sketch entirely in graduated tones without any lines at all, and this can look very effective. It is also a good test of your draughtsmanship because if you are unable to visualise in advance exactly what form the shapes of tone are going to take your sketch will not look right, and if you make any alterations the treatment will lose its freshness.

One of the chief attractions of this type of drawing, like that of a direct water-colour, is the feeling that it was done quite spontaneously, and if there is any erasing or odd bit of tone added afterwards this quality will be lost.

This ' tone only ' method of sketching is of special advantage to people whose work is inclined to be a bit ' tight ' or finicky as there is no opportunity to put a lot of fussy, careful linework or unnecessary detail into the picture. One just has to take the bull by the horns and go straight ahead with the broad essentials.

MOVEMENT

I F you are drawing craft in harbour, or a sailing vessel becalmed, there will be little appreciable movement, and the result is a quiet, peaceful view. But a fishing craft under way at full speed or sailing in a fresh breeze is full of life and movement, and it is important to convey this in your sketch because few things look worse than a subject supposed to be moving but which, in the drawing, is dull and lifeless.

In ship drawing it is mainly the formation of the sea immediately around the vessel that gives an effect of movement. Also the straining of the sails in a wind-driven craft, and smoke from a steamer's funnel are secondary items which help to build up the impression of speed. Predominantly horizontal lines in the sky will add a little too.

An amount of water, equal in volume to the submerged part of the hull, is displaced by a ship as she is driven through the sea. This rapid cleaving of the water at the bow and its closing in again at the stern cause wave formation and a disturbance of the surface level along the vessel's sides. The usual small ship form, such as that of a trawler, makes the water pile up at the bows into an arrow-shaped wave which spreads

out on either side. Immediately behind this is a deep hollow, then usually a long, rounded second wave, and lastly a rise in the surface as the water runs free up the under slope of the stern.

Of course in a rough sea this normal effect of displacement is more or less upset by natural waves, and the behaviour of a craft under these conditions requires further study. The way she plunges into an on-coming sea, throwing a cloud of spray over her forecastle; then how she lifts her bow high in the air, while the sea pours off her deck in white

cascades as she shakes herself free, ready to meet the next wave : the manner of a vessel's rolling in a broadside sea ; her behaviour in a swell while lying stopped or at anchor ; how a sailing craft is pressed down by the force of the wind on her canvas. Any of these things may be a vital part of a picture you will want to paint one day, for no matter how well you draw your craft, if she does not appear to fit naturally into the condition of the sea around her, the sketch will be a failure.

METHODS OF FISHING

AT first glance it may seem unnecessary to include a description of fishing methods in a book on drawing the boats. But there are many pitfalls awaiting the artist who tries to construct his own pictures of fishing craft at work without knowing at least something about the technicalities of the fisherman's trade. For instance, after sketching a group of steam drifters in a harbour, he might unknowingly picture them at sea towing their nets trawler fashion, or with their foremasts up as they were in port. Even when sketching 'on the spot' the artist who knows the 'anatomy' of his subject has a great advantage over the man who just draws what he sees—or thinks he sees.

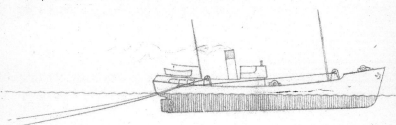

TRAWLING WITH OTTER TRAWL

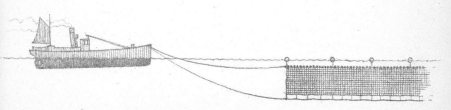

DRIFTER RIDING TO HER NETS

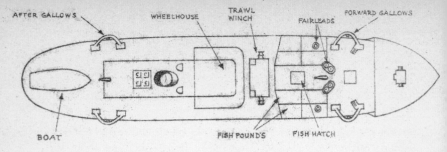

DECK LAYOUT OF A MODERN TRAWLER

To the layman, at a distance, a trawler's deck with all its queerly shaped gear presents a completely meaningless conglomeration of shapes in light and shade, and he will inevitably transfer his lack of knowledge to the paper. On the other hand, an artist who really knows what he is drawing, whilst putting no more detail into his work, can suggest the winch, trawl beam or fairlead with a few deft strokes, in rather the same way as an experienced figure artist moulds a face over the muscle and bone structure he knows to be under the surface.

There are three main methods of net fishing from craft, the most important of which is trawling. The modern ship tows an ' otter trawl ' —a large conical net whose mouth is held open by otter boards. These are like water kites, depending for their action on the angle between the

Otter trawl net

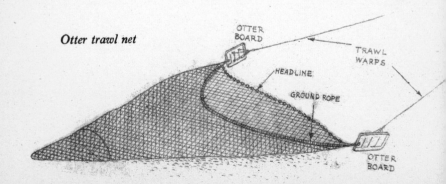

OTTER BOARD

TRAWL WARPS

HEADLINE

GROUND ROPE

OTTER BOARD

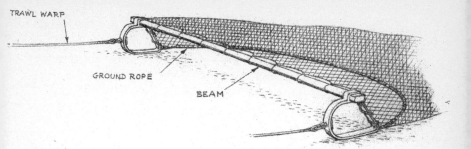

TRAWL WARP

GROUND ROPE

BEAM

boards and the towing warps. The warps are led from the trawl winch, through fairleads and over *one side* of the ship through the fore and after gallows. Some small, old type sailing and auxiliary craft use the ' beam trawl ' in which the net is held open by a heavy wooden beam, raised off the sea bed on ' D ' shaped iron frames.

Drift net fishing is employed for herring, and the steam or motor drifter is an essentially British type of craft. Fleets of these vessels follow the seasonal movement of the herring shoals around our coasts. A long series of vertical nets is paid out, their top edge supported by floats, and the drifter lies stopped, bows on to the nets, drifting. The foremast is lowered and a small sail is set which helps to keep the ship head to wind. The fish are caught by their gills in the fine mesh.

Beam trawl on deck

The ' seine ' net, in various forms, is used in many parts of the world including the American Pacific coast, Scandinavia and S. Africa. In this method a net, supported by floats, is laid round a shoal of fish. The two ends are then hauled in until the fish are imprisoned in a small space in the middle of the net, which is deeper than the ends.

Other methods are ' long line,' consisting of a large number of hooks on a buoyed line perhaps several miles in length ; ' trolling ' that is a craft trailing a number of lines with several hooks on each ; harpooning, either by hand or gun.

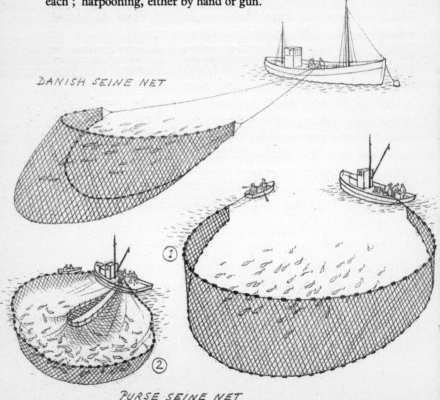

DANISH SEINE NET

PURSE SEINE NET

Hauling Drift Nets

YH 2

TYPES OF CRAFT

THERE are so many fishing craft types throughout the world that it would be impossible to do more than show a very few, selected at random. It is hoped that those on the following pages will serve to illustrate something of the immense variety to be found in this field of marine sketching. There are vessels which have been gradually developed, and are direct descendants from some primitive craft that braved the storms and hardships of the sea many hundreds of years ago. Thousands of fisherman have, from time to time, added or altered small details according to their individual ideas and experience of local conditions. Sometimes accidental contact with the boats of another country has meant the adoption of some method of construction or design that the fisherman considered better than his own. So the boat has grown into the best craft for her purpose.

On the other hand some types, such as the whale factory ship and steam whale catcher, are comparatively new, while the building of special ships for the processing and deep freezing of fish caught by a fleet of accompanying trawlers is a possibility in the near future.

Incidentally, lest anyone should feel like pointing out that whales are mammals, not fish, I may as well say that this is realised, but whalers have been included because their job is, to all intents and purposes, a form of fishing.

STEAM AND MOTOR TRAWLERS

I N the early days of sailing trawlers a harbour would sometimes be crowded with fishing smacks, and in head winds or calms it was very difficult for them to get out of the harbour mouth until the advent of the first steam powered paddle tugs.

The fleets soon saw the great advantage of this development and one tug might be seen towing three or four smacks to sea at a time.

Then somebody had the idea of towing a net from the tug herself. Many paddle tugs were converted for trawling, like the one in my sketch, which incidentally is a black-and-white wash drawing.

After this, vessels with steam power were designed specially for the work, and the steam trawler was born from which the highly efficient ships of to-day have been developed.

Paddle tug converted for trawling —

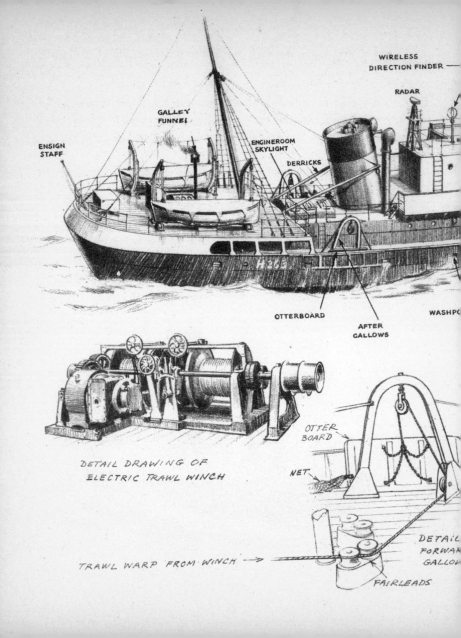

WIRELESS
DIRECTION FINDER

RADAR

GALLEY
FUNNEL

ENGINEROOM
SKYLIGHT

DERRICKS

ENSIGN
STAFF

OTTERBOARD

AFTER
GALLOWS

WASHPO

DETAIL DRAWING OF
ELECTRIC TRAWL WINCH

OTTER
BOARD

NET

DETAIL
FORWA
GALLO

TRAWL WARP FROM WINCH →

FAIRLEADS

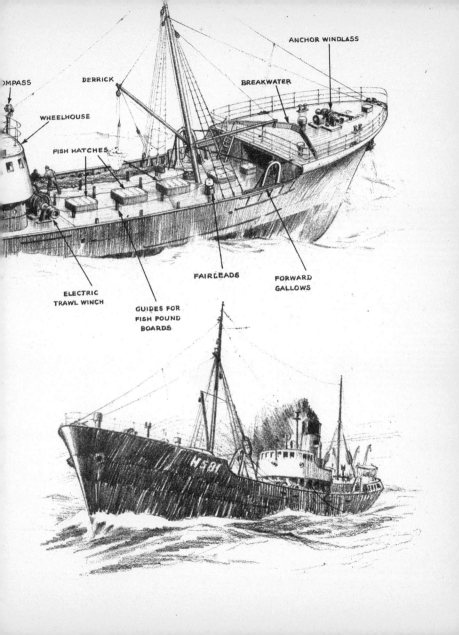

COMPASS

WHEELHOUSE

DERRICK

ANCHOR WINDLASS

BREAKWATER

FISH HATCHES

ELECTRIC
TRAWL WINCH

GUIDES FOR
FISH POUND
BOARDS

FAIRLEADS

FORWARD
GALLOWS

British "New Look" steam trawler

Orthodox Icelandic steam trawler

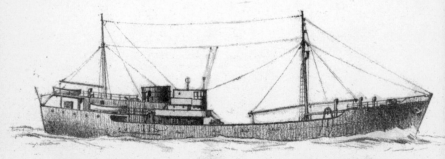

Spanish Newfoundland Banks motor trawler

All steam and motor vessels using the otter trawl have very much the same deck layout. The general arrangement can be seen in the drawing on pages 40 and 41, to which the names of the principal items have been added. There is considerable variation in size and certain features of design but the relative positions of the working deck fittings and gear remain similar for all classes of vessel.

Old type
Steam Trawler

Not so many years ago steam trawlers had a vertical stem, very tall thin funnel and two masts. The profile of a modern British trawler with her raked stem, single mast and squat, tapering funnel shows the great change which has taken place in the appearance of these vessels. Diesel engines are becoming ever more widely used, and the large Spanish motor trawler illustrates a modern ship typical of her class. Below is a little Boulogne motor trawler seen in Ramsgate harbour in 1952. This shows how craft may sometimes be found in unexpected places.

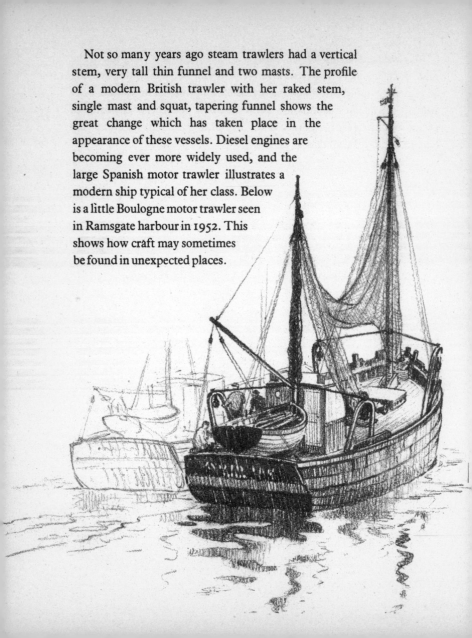

SPANISH 'PAREJA' TRAWLER

THE Pareja or 'Pair' fishing craft are so námed because two boats steer parallel courses towing a large net between them. The ships themselves serve the same purpose as the otter boards of trawlers using that method, keeping the mouth of the net stretched wide. In appearance they are rather like the ordinary small steam trawler, but have an unbroken and more pronounced sheer line. Some are now motor driven, having the same hull form but not the tall funnel. Their work is carried on mainly in the Biscay area.

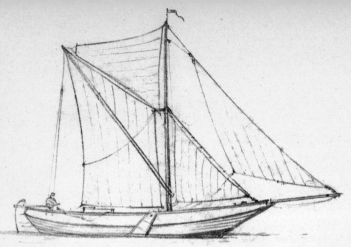

DUTCH CRAFT

Above is a Hoogart employed in mussel fishing from Walcheren. She has a sprit rig, like the Thames barge. The sketch below, made at Flushing, shows another typically Dutch vessel fitted with otter trawl gear. Her decorative rudder head and tiller is inset.

46

HASTINGS LUGGER

A sturdy boat working from the open beach. A conspicuous feature is the 'lute' stern. Her method of fishing is with a beam trawl. The sketch is not an accurate, detailed drawing but a very free impression of the craft.

Note rudder hauled up. Rudder head and tackle for raising can be seen above trawl beam.

Steam Drifters –

STEAM DRIFTERS

THE great majority of drifters are steam-driven at the present time, although motor craft are on the increase. In general appearance they are not unlike small steam trawlers. The superstructure is roughly the same, including the funnel and stokehold ventilators. A small boat is on deck aft. But the trawl winch is absent. Instead, there is a power-driven capstan for hauling the nets, their warps coming in over the bow. The capstan is close to the foremast, on the starboard side (an exception to the rule about fittings being on or equidistant from the centre line). The mast is fitted for lowering in such a way that its upper end rests on the top of the wheelhouse. There are no gallows, and the fish pounds are simpler than a trawler's.

A characteristic of these craft is that the mizzen mast is more or less vertical, although the funnel is raked.

Steam Drifter on slipway at Lowestoft.

BAWLEYS

Outstanding points about this little Thames shrimper are a very long topmast and gaff. The mainsail has no boom and can be 'brailed' in to the mastlike that of a Thames barge. Sketch below shows Leigh cocklers, similar boats, but now fitted with engines ; they seldom use sail.

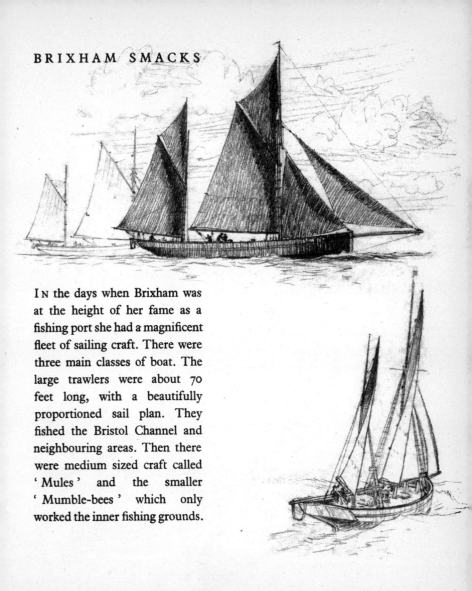

BRIXHAM SMACKS

IN the days when Brixham was at the height of her fame as a fishing port she had a magnificent fleet of sailing craft. There were three main classes of boat. The large trawlers were about 70 feet long, with a beautifully proportioned sail plan. They fished the Bristol Channel and neighbouring areas. Then there were medium sized craft called 'Mules' and the smaller 'Mumble-bees' which only worked the inner fishing grounds.

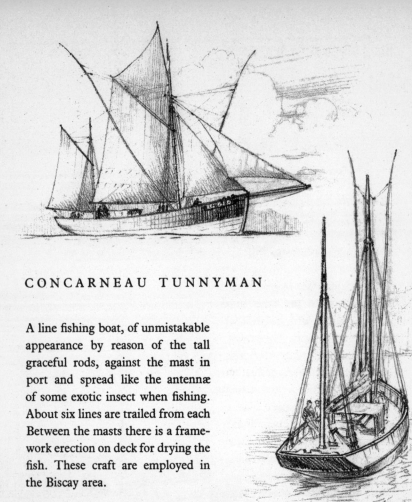

CONCARNEAU TUNNYMAN

A line fishing boat, of unmistakable
appearance by reason of the tall
graceful rods, against the mast in
port and spread like the antennæ
of some exotic insect when fishing.
About six lines are trailed from each
Between the masts there is a frame-
work erection on deck for drying the
fish. These craft are employed in
the Biscay area.

52

SEINE NET FISHERS

THESE craft vary a great deal in different parts of the world as shown by my two examples.

Above is a modern, diesel driven boat from S. Africa. Her mast and all superstructure are well forward because fishing gear and catch are handled from the stern. She employs a 'purse' seine net. In this method the bottom edge of the net is gathered in under the fish when hauling.

The sketch at the right is of a Scandinavian seine netter. She is a wooden ship with motor engine, registered at Lysekil, on the Swedish west coast. There many Danish boats very similar in appearance.

LL 757

NEWFOUNDLAND BANKS SCHOONERS

THESE graceful ships are wooden built and have almost yacht-like lines. There were some beautiful shots of them at sea in the film *Captains Courageous*. Fishing is from dories, which are flat-bottomed open boats. Long lines with a large number of baited hooks are used.

About a dozen dories are carried on the deck of the schooner, and their particular shape allows them to be stowed one inside the other, saving valuable space. On arrival at the fishing grounds the dories are put over the side with two men in each, and spread out around the parent ship, which keeps a motherly eye on them in case of sudden bad weather or accident. Some schooners, with motor engines and masts cut short, still carry on the cod fishing, although they have been joined and will soon be superseded by modern steel motor vessels.

WITH THE WHALERS

ANTARCTIC whaling employs two widely different ship types—
the factory ship, of perhaps 20,000 tons, and an accompanying fleet of
catchers. The former is somewhat like an oil tanker, but with the bridge
pushed well forward and twin funnels allowing a tunnel, up which
the whale carcases are hauled on deck, to pass between them. She also
has heavy gantry masts and derricks.

As may be seen, the catcher has very much the general lines of a
trawler, but her more extensive superstructure is carried further
forward and a gangway connects the bridge with a platform at the

bow, on which a harpoon gun is mounted. High on her foremast is a crow's-nest so that a good lookout can be kept for the first sight of a whale spouting.

In my sketch, several carcases may be seen alongside, inflated by compressed air to prevent them sinking.

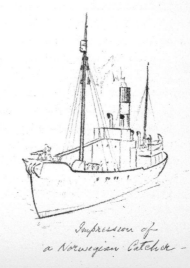

Impression of a Norwegian Catcher —

SURROUNDINGS

THERE are many beautiful or interesting fishing ports and harbours that make a perfect setting for the craft we have been drawing. The havens where fishing vessels lie, and the homes of their crews offer an almost limitless variety of backgrounds.

Large trawler ports have extensive docks and fish quays. The skyline may be broken by the slender arms of cranes or by the austere silhouette and tall chimneys of a factory whose dark smoke overshadows the scene, already hazed by that drifting up from the funnels of countless little ships unloading their catch. Rather a drab subject, you may say, but it is one with the busy grandeur of a great maritime industry.

In the West Country you may find small harbours with worn stone quays, and cottages grouped between red cliffs, soft and warm in colour.

By contrast, Scotland and the North East offer a colder, more severe type of view, grey stone and slate roofs predominating, but possessing their own particular charm. An open beach, un-sheltered and storm-swept is the home of many craft. There will probably be old hand cap-stans for hauling up these boats, and quaint sail lofts or net sheds of weather-stained boarding.

Essex has a number of tiny fishing centres, entirely different again. A narrow creek, winding through salt marshes covered with wiry brown grass and sea lavender, leads to a picturesque village where a little fleet of smacks tug at their moorings and one or two lie up on a miniature 'hard,' being painted. Should one be lucky enough to go abroad there are the gaily painted waterside houses of Holland ; neat wooden buildings backed by towering mountains reflected in the still water of a Norwegian fjord. In short, enough material for a lifetime's work is, one might say, at your pencil point. But much that is interesting and attractive is gradually following the sailing craft themselves into the ever devouring maw of industrial progress. So do not delay too long or where now stands a subject to delight any artist you may find only a desert of steel and concrete.

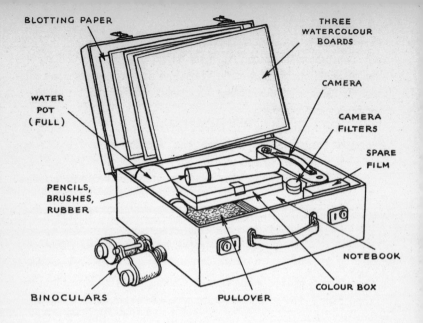

BLOTTING PAPER

THREE
WATERCOLOUR
BOARDS

WATER
POT
(FULL)

CAMERA

CAMERA
FILTERS

SPARE
FILM

PENCILS,
BRUSHES,
RUBBER

NOTEBOOK

BINOCULARS

PULLOVER

COLOUR BOX

SKETCHING OUTFITS

A few words about necessary impedimenta on sketching expeditions. This subject is, of course, largely a matter of personal tastes and requirements; the following suggestions are just my own fads and fancies.

Working among fishing craft in docks or harbours may necessitate clambering over ships' decks, scaling vertical ladders, running across lock gates as they are about to open, or jumping uncomfortable gaps between trawler and quayside. Therefore many of the more elaborate gadgets, such as easels and folding stools should be dispensed with for ordinary, catch-as-catch-can outings. I usually work in pencil, water colour or pen and ink. After various experiments my gear has been reduced to one small leather attache case 14 × 10 × 4½ inches it has a steel frame which makes it strong enough to be turned on end and used as a seat. The following list of contents may seem rather long for such a small case, but they *do* all fit in very nicely.

Pencils, water-colour brushes, pen, rubber, colour box, water bottle, ink, notebook, blotting paper, camera, camera filters, spare film, spare pullover, three sketching boards 13 × 9 inches, binoculars, sandwiches. Colour sketching boards should be light in weight and rigid. The ordinary water-colour board that one can buy is stiff but rather heavy.

Very thick hand-made paper, unmounted, is good to work on but not so rigid, and therefore inclined to flap about on a windy day. It is possible to get corrugated card, brown-paper-faced on both sides. Medium weight water-colour paper stretched over both sides of this, held in place by adhesive strip round the edges, makes an extremely light, rigid board and allows two sketches to be made on one sheet. They are easily stripped off on completion. I find it quite comfortable to work with the board held at a suitable angle between the knees.

The battered old camera is packed because if one has only limited time on a sketch it is sometimes an advantage to take a snap or two of odd details for future reference when finishing the picture at home.

Binoculars are occasionally useful when exploring a strange district, as you can take a long range look at some place a couple of miles away and judge whether it is interesting enough to warrant a visit. They will also reveal details of a distant craft.

By the way, there always may be a particularly awkward ladder or ship's side to climb, and I carry a length of cord in my pocket so that the case may be temporarily slung on my back leaving both hands free.

FISHING PORTS

THE artist who takes up fishing craft as a subject may at first be at a loss to know where to go for first-hand sketches of the boats. Below is a list of just a very few places in Great Britain, with the types of craft likely to be found there. Each fishery area has its special registration letters which are painted on the boats, and these are shewn in brackets :

HULL (H)	
GRIMSBY (GY)	
FLEETWOOD (FD)	Large modern trawlers
MILFORD (M)	
WICK (WK)	
PENZANCE (PZ)	Sailing and auxiliary craft
ABERDEEN (A)	
LOWESTOFT (LT)	Steam drifters, trawlers and
PETERHEAD (PD)	auxiliary engined craft
COLCHESTER (CK)	Small sailing and auxiliary boats
MALDON (MN)	of local type
HASTINGS (X)	Auxiliary and motor craft
(Rye area letters)	launched from the beach

There are, of course, many other fishing centres too numerous to mention, but the reader will probably be able to find out the most convenient to himself, according to where he lives and the type of craft he wants to draw.

CONCLUSION

WHEN people are watching an expert musician or conjuror, or looking at an experienced artist's work, they often say ' It looks so easy.' So it does, and to a certain extent it *is* easy, but that is only because the artist has spent many years in study and practice, gradually increasing his knowledge and improving his technique until any ordinary work that comes within his scope is more or less plain sailing. He can execute it without any doubt or hesitation, confidently tackling all the difficulties of the job with a speed and sureness of line or brush stroke that amaze the layman.

If you feel that some of the drawings in this book ' look easy ' remember that they are in a way built on invisible foundations. These foundations are sacks full of waste paper. On the paper are hundreds of bad and not quite so bad sketches which I have made over a period of many years. They are cemented together by a mortar made of lucky chances, bitter disappointments, occasional successes and perseverance.

This is the experience of almost every artist. He may spend a long time on a drawing and work himself to exhaustion, then throw it away in disgust. But he will have learnt something in the process, and will not make all the same mistakes again.

I only mention this so that, if at first you get your curves all wrong and your boats look twisted out of shape, you will not despair but have another go—and another and another until the difficulties are mastered.

GOING ASHORE